Shall Negro Majorities Rule

John Tyler Morgan

I0102018

ISBN: 978-1-63923-814-9

Printed: March 2023

Published and Distributed By:
Lushena Books
607 Country Club Drive, Unit E
Bensenville, IL 60106
www.lushenabks.com

ISBN: 978-1-63923-814-9

SHALL NEGRO MAJORITIES RULE?

THE population of the United States is made up, mainly, of two races of men, the Caucasian and the African, more than one-seventh being of the latter. In thirteen contiguous States nearly 40 per cent. of the inhabitants are Negroes. In three States the Negroes outnumber the whites. In all political matters the law declares these races to be equal, and secures to men of each all the rights, privileges, and immunities of citizenship that belong to men of the other. In the relations of these races, so different from each other in mental, moral, and physical characteristics, is the "Negro question," which is now receiving, and will hereafter demand in greater degree, the most serious consideration of thinking men of every class and of all sections of the country. In its calm, considerate, and courageons treatment from time to time as it presents itself for action is involved the welfare and tranquillity of both races, and no one who rightly estimates its difficulties and importance will approach a discussion of it in any prejudiced or partisan temper. For twenty years politicians have been playing with it as children with fire, gaining nothing themselves and aggravating a situation fraught with danger from the beginning. There are indications that its gravity is now impressing itself on the minds of men of broad views and serious purpose, who begin to realize that much more is at stake than the gain or loss of the doubtful political advantages of inconsequential party conflicts, and who manifest a disposition to study and investigate it in a fearless, earnest, and patriotic spirit. In any honest consideration of this question one must confront unpleasant facts at the very outset, and these will multiply as inquiry progresses.

It is a question of race conflict. In whatever connection it is considered, whether in church or social relations, in business, professional, or industrial employments, or in politics, it is a matter of race. Every result that we have reached, or that we

:cling." For him, virtues are founded upon expediency; not ideed upon a direct calculation of what is expedient, but upon le registration of it in the human organism. But if morality is ot a formal law, absolute as are the laws of mathematics, trans- ending all persons and all conditions, and sovereignly obligatory pon all, without regard to its consequences and without refer- nce to any personal end—if, I say, it is not all this, it is noth- ig. And as I look around the world I find only too abundant vidence how fast it is becoming nothing in some of the most im- ortant provinces of man's activity, through the debased concep- on of it which the new philosophy has diffused. I have not ow in view individual deflections from the moral code. Whether nose deflections are more or less numerous at one time than nother, is a question of comparatively small importance, if the lea upon which this code rests is generally acknowledged and evered; for then there is always left a principle of recovery. 3ut if that idea falls into discredit, and loses its hold upon the opular mind, the civilization based upon it is c rtainly doomed. ant, if I may again quote him—and assuredly I may, for he, of ll the teachers of our age, has a right to be heard in this con- ection—Kant speaks in a famous passage of "the wonderful lea of duty, self-sustained in the soul by its own bare law, and ver compelling respect, if not always securing obedience." But is respect must vanish—and vanishing it is—when duty is ac- ounted merely the fashion of apprehending that "adjustment of :ternal relations to internal relations" called life; when the tegorical imperative is explained by inbred selfishness *plus* e fear of the constable; when comfort or agreeable feeling exhibited as the ultimate rule of ethics. The philosophy of lativity empties truth of its old meaning. And in every de- irtment of human activity I note the invalidation of the moral lea as this philosophy wins its way into popular acceptation. verywhere I discern tokens of the lowering of the ethical andard. I find them in art. I find them in journalism. I find iem in politics. I find them in the view commonly taken of iat penal law which is, in a true sense, the bond of civil society. propose to consider these several subjects in future numbers of iis review.

W. S. LILLY.

can reach, whether it has been worked out by the Negroes in their natural progress, or by the whites in their endeavors to elevate the Negroes, is a consequence of race conflict. Neither race is responsible for the conditions that make this conflict instinctive and irreconcilable, and neither can avoid the issue or its consequences under the circumstances in which both are placed.

These races, brought together here on terms of political equality, are not equal or homogeneous. Their amalgamation is impossible, because it is forbidden by the instincts of both. The whites of the United States have been remarkably firm and persistent in their insistence upon the maintenance of race distinctions in everything that relates to social existence and progress, and the Negroes have as distinctly shown their aversion to any relaxation of race ties and exclusiveness. The aversion is mutual, and, in a general sense, fixed.

Our native Indians are a strong race, mentally and physically. Many examples of the highest ability in military and civil government have been furnished in the history of the tribes of Indians. With unquestioned capacity for the highest attainment in civil government, they have rejected, practically, every effort we have made to incorporate and identify them with our civil polity. The pride of race, attachment to tribal relations, the ties of kindred, and the craving for the powers of independent self-government have caused them to refuse our most sincere endeavors to raise them to the plane of our civilization. The pride of race has always lived in every Indian's blood, and is now the only remaining element of his former power. Intermarriage with Indians has not been regarded by the whites as in derogation of race, nor is amalgamation of the races forbidden by any recognized natural law, or made impossible by any distinct and admitted aversion; but even with this advantage, very little impression has been made on the Indians toward inducing them to any relaxation of their pride of race in social or governmental affairs. They remain unaffected by the relations and intercourse of centuries, at enmity with our civilization, and in conflict with the whites. Race aversion, amounting to hatred, exists also between the whites and the Chinese. Recent legislation in Congress proves this, if proof were needed. Between these inferior races, also, the division is as marked and the repulsion as decided as it is between either of them and the whites.

Between the African and the white race the bar to union is still more absolute. To remove it, if it could be removed, would be to lower the whites to the level of the intellectual, moral, and social condition of the Negroes. It would be to destroy the white race. One drop of Negro blood known to exist in the veins of a woman in this country draws her down to the social status of the Negro, and impresses upon her whole life the stamp of the fateful Negro caste, though she may rival the Easter lily in the whiteness of her skin. The Negroes, though they may accept almost any form of association with the whites, are never satisfied with any admixture of the blood of the races. It relaxes the hold of their own race upon their affections. Negroes of mixed blood are inferior among the race to which they belong.

It is irrational to attribute these race antipathies and aversions to the laws of this country or to anything in the manner of their administration and enforcement. They rest upon foundations that men have not built, and are supported by ordinances that human power can neither enact nor amend nor repeal. After we have done all that we can to abolish or to neutralize these race distinctions and the feelings that grow out of them—attempting to set aside the eternal laws of nature—we shall find that we have only marked more plainly the differences between the races, and that we have rooted race prejudices more deeply in the hearts of the inferior races and the whites, at least so far as the Chinese and Negroes are concerned. The Negro question is not, therefore, a southern question, but a race question, that appears in every phase of human existence as distinctly in the North, wherever a considerable number of Negroes is found, as in the South.

The personal relations between the Negroes and the white people are more friendly in the South than in the North, because in the South they are based upon the recognition, by both races, of the leadership and superiority of the white race. This recognition of a natural and obvious fact is not offensive to the Negroes, and the relations that accord with it are not constrained or disagreeable to either race.

The southern white man, from long association with the Negroes as a dependent and inferior race, can afford to indulge for them an honest and cordial regard; while the white man in the North feels that, in any exhibition of regard for the Negro, he is sacrificing the dignity of his race and making a personal condescension. He is willing to punish himself with a certain self-abasement to prove to the Negro that he is no more than his equal, while the Negro is compelled to lower his opinion of the white man in order to believe what he says.

If these race instincts and proclivities are wrong, and appeal to humanity for their correction, it by no means follows that the remedy is to be found within the domain of the legislative power, either State or federal. As our Constitution carefully reserves the settlement of all religious and social questions within the great mass of powers that were never surrendered to any government, but were retained by the people, we must look to those powers and to the arbitrament of the people, through the ordinances of public opinion, for the safe and final settlement of race questions in our country. The most serious and important questions connected with the African race will be settled in the "high chancery" of public opinion. When we come to make laws for the regulation of the political powers accorded to the African race, this important factor—public opinion—cannot be disregarded. Without its support such laws will fail of their purpose, however they may be sustained by force. Public opinion, in any part of the United States, will ultimately neutralize statutes that violate the instincts of the white race.

The 13th, 14th, and 15th Amendments of the Constitution of the United States placed the entire Negro population, in the States, in their basis of national representation. They also gave to the Negroes entitled to vote under the permission of State laws, a guarantee that such permission should not be withheld by the States "on account of race, color, or previous condition of servitude." Each of the States conferred upon Negro men of a certain age the privilege of voting. The Negroes thus enfranchised were selected and set apart by the State laws as voters, without any personal selection based on merit or capacity, and were indued with power to influence the destiny of the whole country through their votes. This is the extent to which this subject was pushed by the law-making power. As this privilege of voting was the only political power that was conferred upon any class of Negroes under these laws, that is the only point at which the legislative authority of the country can be exercised rightfully in favor of the Negroes as a race or class of people.

The personal rights of the people of all races and classes are secured alike under our Constitution and laws, but a designated class of the Negro race is the only class of that race in whose favor there is any pretense of the existence of any special power or duty of legislation. The political privilege given to this limited number of Negroes contains the whole subject upon which Congress could legislate, if it has any power to regulate the voting of Negroes or white people in the States. The question of the safety of the Negro race is not involved in this controversy, unless we insist that Negro voters alone can protect the rights of the Negro race. The Negro question relates only to the political power of those Negroes who have the privilege of voting under the State laws. They constitute about one-fifth of the Negro population. The other four-fifths are no more interested personally in preserving the ballot in the hands of the Negro voter than are so many white people. With one-fifth it is a privilege; with the remaining four-fifths it is only a sentiment, or question of race.

The States have the exclusive right to prescribe the qualifications of voters. They are prohibited from giving any preference to a white voter over a Negro voter, but they may give such preference to the white voter over the Indian or Chinaman, even if he is a citizen. Without the assistance of the laws of the States, respectively, the right of suffrage could not be completely exercised. If we grant, for the sake of the argument, that Congress may legislate in favor of the right of the Negro to vote in certain elections, still the support of the people is as much needed to enforce that legislation as if it were a law of the State. Without this sustaining sentiment any law will fail. Coercion may, for a time, repress the practical expression of public sentiment, but such pressure must ultimately cease. However great it may be, it will only intensify opposition to laws that are in hostility to the settled convictions of the white race in this country. The reaction of public opinion against such laws usually results in thoroughly removing the subject from further controversy. It is certain that no law can long be enforced among a people as free as ours when their opposition to it is sincere. This is especially true when such laws demand the humiliation of the white race, or the admission of the Negroes to a dangerous participation, as a race, in the affairs of our government.

Each voter in this country represents a group of five persons, including himself. In his selection as the trustee of such power, the law alone speaks. Nobody selects him; in many instances nobody would select him as a representative, and he is not in the least responsible to those he represents for his opinions or conduct. The remaining four persons of the group, who are excluded from voting, have no sort of control over their representative, except through the influence of public opinion. This is therefore the only check upon the representative voters, who are otherwise more autocratic in their powers than any other class of men in the world. In the States of this Union, 13,000,000 of men rule 65,000,000 of people in everything that relates to the making of laws and the choice of all the officers concerned in government, whether civil or military. If we could silence the press and repress the utterances of the people, leaving the control of our destiny solely to the uninstructed and unrestrained will of the voting class, our liberties would perish in the hands of our guardians, created by law; and "the people," who are the natural guardians of the country, would find no means through which to exert the powers reserved to them in the Constitution. Public opinion is, at last, the mightiest agency in free self-government, and it will ultimately dispose of the Negro question according to the enlightened judgment and the will of the white race in the United States.

It is not in the power of man to bring about a general infusion of the blood of the Negro race into that of the white race, and with this infusion to Africanize our people in their social instincts and in their ideas of government. The common law of Africa, which is slavery, cannot be substituted in the United States for the common law of England, which is liberty, and which is to us as much an inheritance as slavery is to the African race. Public opinion will never sanction so radical a change in the condition and relations of these races in this country, and all the laws, of whatever dignity, that look in that direction will fail of their purpose. The votes of the Negroes will be arrayed in constant opposition to this sentiment and resolution of the white race, but they will never reverse this current of public opinion. They will only increase and strengthen it.

The laws that give the ballot to one-fifth of the Negro race appeal to the race prejudice which incites them to persistent effort to accomplish the impossible result of race equality. "Equality before the law" is the phrase in which this demand is expressed, but this condition is impossible without equality in the opinion and conscience of the white race. The question is the same in every State, North or South, where any considerable body of Negroes is found, and the decree of public opinion is the same.

The Negroes are no more capable than we are of setting aside the natural influence of race. The honest Negro will vote with his race at every opportunity, just as the honest white man will vote with his. Every sentiment and affection of the human heart is engaged in behalf of the race to which the voter belongs. It is impossible that any man can vote impartially when a question is presented in which his race is believed to be vitally concerned, and it is folly to expect such a vote. The sentiment or public opinion of his race will control him beyond his power of resistance. Education, refinement, wealth, and the consciousness of personal merit add a stronger jealousy to the power of race, and continually widen the separation between the white and Negro races. This effect is more decided with the Negro than it is with the white race. It has increased every day since the Negroes were emancipated. They demand, with greater earnestness than ever before, that their representatives shall be Negroes, and not white men. No solidity of political affiliation can resist this burrowing suspicion of the Negro race that a white man is the natural enemy of the Negro power in government.

We have not accomplished any good to either race by conferring upon 1,500,000 Negroes the privilege of voting. Its effect is only to neutralize the same number of white votes that would otherwise be cast with reference to the general welfare and prosperity of the country. It is needless to recall the history of the race contests that have pervaded the ballot-box under this mistaken policy. The facts are present, in every election, to establish the existence of this national misfortune. Unless the voter can sink his race proclivities and aversions in his sense of duty to his country, it is in vain that we endeavor to compel by law the harmonious action of the white and Negro races, either in voting or in conducting the government. This impossible condition is hidden in the core of the Negro question, and neither law-makers, judges, nor executive officers can remove it.

Whether the aversion and incongruity of the races is the result of slavery in the United States or of slavery in Africa, whether it dates back two centuries or ten, it is fixed and irreconcilable. No human law created this condition and none can destroy it. All the laws we can enact of a coercive or compulsory character will only intensify this aversion. They will only force the races wider apart the more we attempt to compel their accord, or their union into a homogeneous society or into political fellowship.

As to the domination of the Negro race in the government of any State of this Union, the American people have already decreed that it is impossible. As to the control of the government of any State by a few self-seeking white men, supported by the votes of the Negroes as a class, acting, as they would do, upon their race instincts and aversions, the impracticability of such a plan has already been demonstrated. That experiment has cost the country too dearly to admit of its being tried again. We may take the history of the Negro in politics for the last twenty years as a fair indication of the future influence of that race in our government, and it is not likely to increase in the ratio of the growth of that class of population. By whatever means their political influence has been reduced, even if it has been unlawfully reduced, it shows a want of governing power in that race that makes it a hopeless undertaking to place them in supremacy over the white race. Increase their numbers as we may in any State or political division, and leave to the Negroes alone the working out of the result, yet they will fail to achieve the political control of the white people. Unite with them enough of the organizing and governing power of the white race to enable them to reach a desired result in the elections or in legislation, and it will be temporary and fruitless. Their jealousy of the white men, or of the mulattoes, whom they permit to help them into power, always leads them to dismiss both as soon as possible from their confidence and support. They go overboard, and the Negro takes the helm. The men who lend themselves to the Negro race for such purposes perish in reputation under the silent condemnation of the white race, in virtue of a law of public opinion that they cannot escape.

Outside pressure from people who are in no immediate danger and have nothing at stake but their sentiments of justice or philanthropy, cannot change the conduct or modify the opinions of those who have at risk and in charge, as a trust imposed upon them by the blood of kindred, all that is sacred in society and in family. Such pressure must result in permanent harm to the Negro race, while it may also seriously injure the white race temporarily. If the laws of the States in reference to elections, of which no complaint is made, are evaded, or if they are not enforced, it is because public opinion sets too strongly against them. Laws of Congress which can be executed only through the assistance of the people of the States would meet a similar fate.

It is not because the southern white people were once slaveholders that the ballot in the hands of the Negro race is regarded by them as a dangerous power. If all the Negroes in South Carolina were transferred to New Hampshire, the people of that State would dread the power of the ballot in their hands far more than the southern ex-slaveholders do. The great body of southern white voters never were slaveholders; but the farther we draw away from the slave era, the greater is the aversion of the white people to Negro rule, and the weaker the Negro becomes in the use of political power. We may attribute this to the perverseness of the white race, and ascribe to the negro the virtue of integrity in his purposes and meek submission in his conduct, if we prefer to revile our own race in order to make excuses for the impotence of the Negroes as a ruling class. But, in that case, it is plainly a hopeless task to reform the white people so as to render them capable of doing justice to the Negroes as joint rulers

of the States, or to elevate the Negro race so as to make them
capable, aside from mere race proclivities and race advantages, of
estimating the privileges and power of the ballot. It is still more
hopeless to attempt to compress into one the races of men that
God has separated into great families, to each of which he gives
the ideas of self-government best suited to its development into a
higher civilization.

The southern people are not mistaken as to the dangers of the
ballot in the hands of the Negro race. Twenty years of experience, beginning with eight years of the horrors of enforced Negro
rule, has demonstrated to them that a relapse into that condition
would be the worst form of destruction. They are no more
amenable to moral censure for attempting to avoid that desperate
fate than are the people who, in all parts of our country, punish
with instant death the Indian or Chinaman or Negro who inflicts
a worse fate than death upon an innocent woman. Congress can
do nothing to prevent such violations of the laws, even in the
Territories and against its wards the Indians and Negroes, or its
protégés the Chinamen. Our history is full of such instances,
where the laws of the United States were violated in spite of the
powers of this great government. Congress has often shrunk
before public opinion in such cases, and has paid the damages to
the sufferers while the violators of the law, thus securely fortified,
have gone scot-free.

Congress is looked to, by ambitious aspirants for office and
power, as the tribunal to furnish the corrective for the alleged de-
linquency of the people of the States in the execution of the State
laws, whereby the Negro is said to be deprived of his suffrage.
If Congress has such powers and can substitute in the States a
body of people who will better execute the laws, there may be a
chance of the success of these interested speculators in political
"futures." But if the substituted people are of the Negro race,
or if they are made up of a combination of the two races, the evident effect would be to inflame the race animosities and aversions, and to base the success of the experiment upon that condition. The Negroes would enter eagerly on this plan because it
would arouse their race instincts, and the white contingent would
join them for purposes of plunder—such as the South suffered in

every public office, and man by man, from 1866 to 1875. The result of this forced combination would be, if it were successful, the domination of the Negro race in the invaded States. They would furnish the power, and their mercenaries would furnish the skill, through which the capture of the State governments would be accomplished. Power thus gained could not be enduring, for the Negro would insist upon the full measure of his rights, and would soon kick his hirelings out of the places of honor and profit. Then the unconquerable power of the white race, if it never raised an arm in forcible resistance to such a degradation, would so express itself through the silent but omnipotent influence of public opinion, that all who fostered such a warfare on the honor of the race would perish. But Congress has no power to force, or to make possible, such a condition of affairs. Passing by, for this occasion, the discussion of the powers of Congress in the control of the ballot in the States, the policy of such an effort would be unwise and fearfully injurious.

If this is a race question that the existing amendments of the Constitution could not settle or suppress, and if it must be solved at last by the will of the people as it shall be expressed either in support of or against the safety of entrusting political power, under our system of government, to the inferior Negro race, the question will be whether the public sentiment, or public opinion, or the laws, which shall furnish the ultimate solution of the problem, shall be those of the people of the States respectively which have this trouble to meet, or whether other States must interfere, through the action of Congress, to settle the matter in all its details.

In support of the proposition that the people of the States respectively should be left free, under the Constitution, to deal with this difficult problem without the interference of other States, it is first assumed, with evident reason, that Congress cannot successfully control the suffrage of the people in the States by any means. Military coercion would only increase the difficulties, and that resort may be dismissed as impossible. Whatever is done to secure to the Negroes the full use of the ballot must be done through State laws and through public opinion in the States. If the belief of the white race is that the enforcement of these laws will destroy their civilization, the laws will not be executed, though the refusal to execute them should cost the States their representation in Congress.

It must be remembered that it was an entire race of people that we enfranchised with the ballot, and not the individuals of that race who may have been personally competent to use it with judgment for the general good of the people. Our process of enfranchising the Indians is just the reverse of this. We make citizens of them, man by man, and upon the condition of their proving their capacity for citizenship by dissolving their tribal relations and taking lands in severalty. A plan looking to some personal fitness of the Negro for the high duties and corresponding powers of citizenship would not have shocked the common sense of the people, and would have collected into the body of voters in the States those Negroes who had at least some idea of the uses and value of the ballot. The plan we adopted, of transferring the whole of this inferior race into the body of our citizenship, with the powers of government, was a rash experiment, that has not succeeded in accomplishing any good to either race.

Unfortunately it was thrust into the Constitution with inconsiderate haste, and we are repenting at our leisure the having dealt with this political and temporary question in the heat of our national animosities, as if it had been an essential part of the liberties of "ourselves and our posterity." Being in the Constitution, it must be respected and obeyed by the States, for that is the injunction and corresponding pledge of every State. But the people will take the liberty of lending their moral and material support to the States in the enforcement of this awful blunder, to the extent and in the degree and in the manner that will cause the least interference with the "rights reserved to the people" in the same Constitution, among which is the right "to secure the blessings of liberty to ourselves and our posterity," and also "to insure domestic tranquillity."

Without the moral and material support of the white people who are affected by the presence of masses of the Negro race, those State laws cannot be enforced which promote the idea of Negro supremacy. This support will never be given, and the opposition to this possible result will be so strong that it will draw within its depressing power the Negro vote and the Negro voter, until the dread of Negro supremacy is dissipated.

If the Negroes can be worked into the representative charac-ter which every voter has, under our laws, as a useful and safe repository of such power, while in their family connections. in all social relations, and in every business pursuit they are doomed to stand apart from the white race as a class condemned to an inferiority of position from which there is no escape, it will be done through the impression they will make on those among whom they live, and not by impressions made through acts of Congress, expressive of the opinions and wishes of people who know but little about them and care less, except as the means of increasing their own political power.

Protestations of good will for the Negro race, when made by southern people, are not accepted as being sincere by those who believe that the ex-slaveholder and his posterity are incapable of sympathy or regard for that race of men. The argument, if applied to the ex-slave-catcher and his posterity, would carry with it much more logical strength. If we compare the condition of the Negro, caught in his native land and enslaved. with that of his posterity in the South as it was at the date of the 13th Amendment, simple justice cannot deny to the former slaveholding South the credit of having dealt far more generously with the Negroes than those who caught them in Africa or bought them from the slave ships.

The southern people do not desire to deprive the Negro race of any power or facility that will make freedom a blessing to them. What they seek to avoid is the consolidation of power in the hands of the Negro race that will be used, through the incentives of race aversion, to put them in control of the govern-ment of the white race.

Agitation in Congress and in political clubs will keep the prospect of such ascendency ever before the Negroes, and will create opposition to the Negro voter that, otherwise, would be of little effect in any respect, and would never endanger the personal rights of that race. If these questions are permitted to await the solution that experience alone can provide, through the conduct. of the people who have befriended this race when they

The safe, benevolent, and wise solution of the Negro question can be left to the people of the States respectively, under the Constitution, with far greater security for every right now accorded to the Negroes, and for every blessing that may follow, than it can be to the politicians and agitators in other States.

JOHN T. MORGAN.

41